Food Dudes

TOM MONAGHAN:

Domino's Pizza Innovator

Sheila Griffin Llanas

Checkerboard
Library

An Imprint of Abdo Publishing
www.abdopublishing.com

www.abdopublishing.com

Published by Abdo Publishing, a division of ABDO, PO Box 398166, Minneapolis, Minnesota 55439. Copyright © 2015 by Abdo Consulting Group, Inc. International copyrights reserved in all countries. No part of this book may be reproduced in any form without written permission from the publisher. Checkerboard Library™ is a trademark and logo of Abdo Publishing.

Printed in the United States of America, North Mankato, Minnesota.
052014
092014

THIS BOOK CONTAINS
RECYCLED MATERIALS

Cover Photos: Corbis
Interior Photos: AP Images pp. 8, 19, 25, 27; Corbis p. 1; Getty Images pp. 5, 10, 11, 13, 15, 23, 24;
    Glow Images p. 9; iStockphoto pp. 7, 17, 21, 26

Series Coordinator: Megan M. Gunderson
Editors: Grace Hansen, Bridget O'Brien
Art Direction: Neil Klinepier

Library of Congress Cataloging-in-Publication Data

Llanas, Sheila Griffin, 1958-
  Tom Monaghan : Domino's Pizza innovator / Sheila Griffin Llanas.
      p. cm. -- (Food dudes)
  Audience: Grade 8-12.
  ISBN 978-1-62403-316-2
1. Monaghan, Tom, 1937---Juvenile literature. 2. Domino's Pizza (Firm)--Juvenile literature. 3. Restaurateurs--United States--Biography--Juvenile literature. 4. Businessmen--United States--Biography--Juvenile literature. I. Title.
  TX910.5.M59L53 2015
  647.95092--dc23
  [B]
                                                    2014006825

Contents

Tom Monaghan

Today, pizza delivery is common. Call the shop and place an order. Wait for a hot pizza to arrive at your home. In the 1960s, delivery was not nearly as common. That's when Tom Monaghan started Domino's Pizza. He built his company on his delivery promise, hot and fresh in 30 minutes.

After that, delivery became the pizza standard. Today, 58,000 of the nation's 70,000 pizzerias offer delivery. Monaghan helped change the food industry. In doing so, he turned his life into a major success.

Thomas Stephen Monaghan was born on March 25, 1937, just outside Ann Arbor, Michigan. He had a younger brother, Jim. Their father, Francis, was a truck driver. Their mother, Anna, was a nurse's aide. The four of them had a happy family life. Then on Christmas Eve 1941, Tom's father died of **peritonitis**. Tom was only four years old.

Tom's mother could not support her children alone. She earned just $27.50 a week. So, she sent her sons to **foster homes** and then St. Joseph's Home for Boys, a Catholic **orphanage**. Tom hated the place! It wasn't fair. He was a good kid with bad luck. Back then, he began to dream of a better life.

Tom Monaghan's big dreams helped him through tough times.

Tough Childhood

Tom was a quick thinker and a good athlete. At first, he did well in the **orphanage**. One teacher, Sister Berarda, asked students about their future goals. Tom said he wanted to be a priest, an **architect**, and a shortstop for the Detroit Tigers baseball team. His classmates laughed. The teacher did not. She said Tom could be whatever he wanted to be. Under her care, Tom's grades were high.

In third grade, Sister Berarda's replacement was very different. She whipped children for the smallest errors. Tom's grades dropped. He began to fail.

Tom spent six and a half awful years at St. Joseph's. Then, he lived with his mother in Traverse City, Michigan. To help her with money, he picked cherries and sold newspapers, vegetables, and fish. Tom tried hard, but he and his mother argued. She said she could not control him.

Tom returned to the **foster care** system. In ninth grade, he lived with the Crouch family. He loved them and was happy to help on their farm. He also began to pursue new interests. In particular, he admired the work of famous architect Frank Lloyd Wright.

The next year, Tom attended a **seminary** in Grand Rapids, Michigan, to become a priest. He was kicked out for bad behavior, and his dream of being a priest was shattered. He returned to living with his mother, but again this did not go well. He was sent to a **detention home**. At the end of eleventh grade, Tom went to live with his aunt and uncle in Ann Arbor.

Traverse City is in the northern part of Michigan's Lower Peninsula.

The Marines

While living with his family, Tom attended St. Thomas High School in Ann Arbor. Tom did not focus on school. He graduated in 1955 only after begging not to be held back. He finished last out of 44 students.

Next, Tom tried college. He attended Ferris State College in Big Rapids, Michigan, for one quarter. There, he achieved good grades. Then, he was accepted at the University of Michigan to study **architecture**. Yet without enough money for **tuition**, he gave up his dream of earning a degree.

In 1956, Tom joined the US Marine Corps. Boot camp was **grueling**! He learned some tough lessons. He got in top shape, both physically

Ferris State College became Ferris State University in 1987.

The Imperial Hotel was torn down in 1968.

and mentally. Tom boarded a ship and crossed the Pacific Ocean to his assignment. All of his spare time went toward self-improvement.

Stationed in Okinawa, Japan, Tom read books on business. While on guard duty, he gazed at the majestic Mount Fuji. He traveled to Tokyo to visit the Imperial Hotel. It was designed by his idol Frank Lloyd Wright. Being a marine was an excellent choice for Tom. The experience boosted his confidence and his sense of self-worth. He vowed to someday find success and make his dreams come true.

The Pizza Biz

Monaghan left the military in 1959. He returned to Ann Arbor, planning to give college another try. Meanwhile, he managed a crew of newspaper deliverers. With this job, he learned a little about business. He also sold subscriptions for the Sunday *New York Times*. Delivering them himself, he earned an extra $25 a week. He worked hard and was able to buy a corner newsstand downtown.

As hard as he worked, Monaghan could not save for **tuition**. College seemed impossible. At 23 years old, Monaghan worried his life was going nowhere. Then one day, his brother, Jim, told him about a pizzeria in Ypsilanti, Michigan. It

When Monaghan entered the pizza industry, he hoped to run a successful business and earn money for college.

was called DomiNick's Pizza, and it was for sale. The Monaghan boys borrowed $900. They bought the small place in 1960.

Monaghan quit his newspaper job. He had no degree and little business experience. He knew nothing about pizza. The previous owner gave him a 15-minute lesson in pizza-making. That was his only training! On December 9, the brothers opened the shop. That night, Monaghan entered the pizza industry.

Monaghan (second from right) *in his early days in the pizza business.*

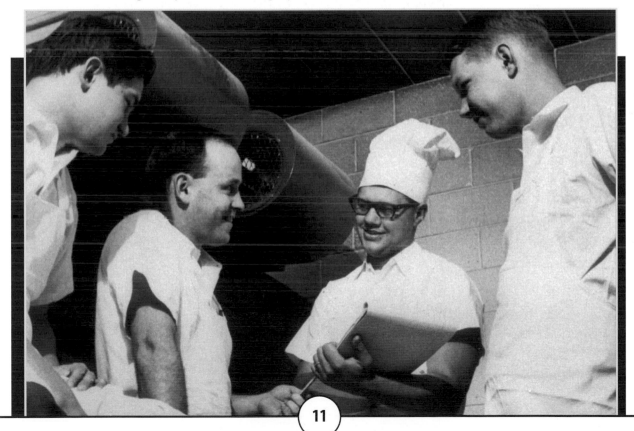

A Low Point

At their pizzeria, the Monaghan brothers shared the work. Yet profits were low. In their first week, they earned just $99. Then after eight months, Jim quit! Monaghan traded the Volkswagen Beetle they used for deliveries for Jim's share of the business. He became the sole owner of DomiNick's in 1961. From then on, Monaghan committed himself fully to pizza.

Monaghan worked day and night, seven days a week. To his surprise, he loved rolling pizza dough. It was rewarding to make delicious tomato sauce. He tried his competitors' pizza to see how he could improve his own. And, he worked hard to make the whole process faster. Yet he had one big problem. His profits remained low and **debts** were piling up.

During one busy night, Monaghan almost gave up. Several employees were absent. Monaghan feared a small crew could not handle the work. Failure seemed certain. He saw only one option, which was to close down the pizza place. Then, an employee suggested a perfect solution.

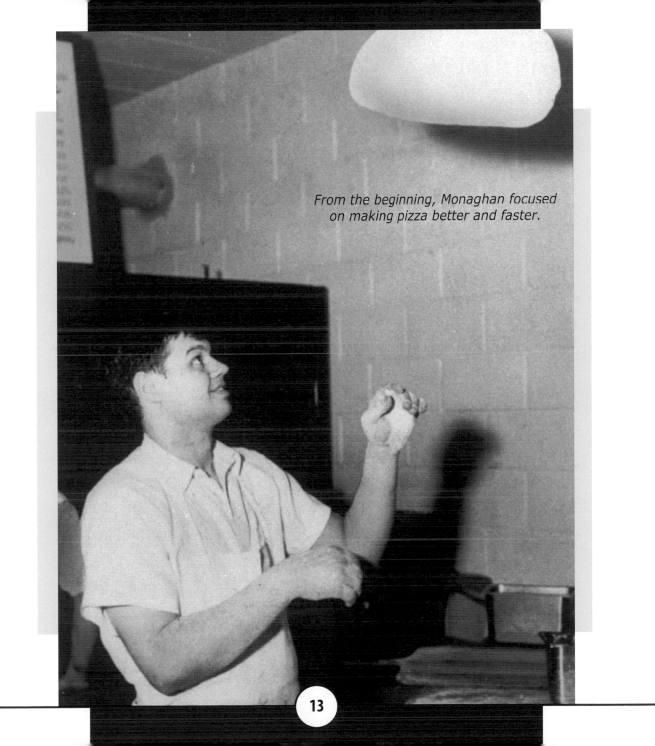

From the beginning, Monaghan focused on making pizza better and faster.

Pizza Principles

On that miserable night, Monaghan made a drastic move. At the time, DomiNick's offered pizza in five sizes. The smallest and most popular was the six-inch pie. It took effort to provide so many choices for customers. Small pizzas took as long to make as large pies. But they cost less. DomiNick's lost money on the smaller size.

With nothing to lose, Monaghan dropped six-inch pizzas from his menu. A few customers complained. But then, they simply chose to pay more for a larger pie! That night, an amazing thing happened. Monaghan's smaller staff filled every pizza order and never fell behind. The operation ran smoothly. Best of all, they made more money than ever, all because they dropped one item from the menu.

Everything changed. Just like that, DomiNick's earned a profit. The next night, Monaghan dropped nine-inch pizzas from the menu. Again, he was amazed. The simpler menu was more profitable. Customers were just as happy. Monaghan had learned an invaluable business lesson. His luck began to change. He was far from rich, but at least he could pay the bills.

Monaghan first tried pizza
in high school. At the
time, he didn't care for it!

A New Name

Based on the menu change, Monaghan created a vision of service. He sold only pizza and nothing else. He offered takeout or delivery with little sit-down service.

DomiNick's had a great location. It was near a college campus. When hunger hit, students wanted food fast! In 1965, Monaghan set a new goal to deliver every order within 30 minutes.

While delivering a pizza to a college campus one night, Monaghan met Marjorie Zybach. On August 25, 1962, they married. At the time, Monaghan was making $102 a week. The couple moved into a cozy, modest trailer home. The Monaghans went on to have four daughters. Mary was born in 1963, followed by Susie in 1965 and Maggie in 1969. The youngest, Barbara, was born in 1972.

Meanwhile, Monaghan expanded his business to include more locations. In Ypsilanti, he had a store called Pizza King. In Ann Arbor, another college town, he owned Pizza from the Prop.

The new Domino's logo had three white dots to represent the three stores Monaghan was running at the time.

Monaghan had never owned rights to the name DomiNick's. So eventually the former owner, Dominick DiVarti, insisted he change it. In 1965, Monaghan settled on Domino's. He loved the Italian sound. A red domino game piece became his new logo. He hoped to add an extra dot for each new store. He had no idea how many locations he would eventually have!

The Pizza Hustle

Monaghan's business was doing well. Each of his new stores sold about 3,000 pizzas a week. And Monaghan was working harder than ever. He hustled from ten each morning to four the next morning! He took off just three days a year, Thanksgiving, Christmas, and Easter.

Monaghan became a **strict** boss. Employees had to show up on time and work hard. In return, they were treated well. Monaghan thought of them as family. In fact, he was best man in the weddings of some of his employees.

Monaghan continued seeking ways to save time. To improve efficiency, he bought new machines to grate and mix the cheese and make dough. He invested in special boxes to store the dough.

Speed was one key to success, but flavor was another. Monaghan conducted undercover street interviews. He asked people where he could find good pizza and whether Domino's was any good. He listened to both positive and negative comments from these secret taste tests. He used their feedback to improve the quality of his food.

Monaghan was busy, but he still had passions outside of pizza. One of them was baseball. In 1968, his beloved Detroit Tigers won the World Series. When the team flew home, fans planned to greet them at the airport. Monaghan decided to surprise the team with Domino's pizzas.

On the drive, he and his employees got stuck in a traffic jam! So, they ran from car to car, selling 100 hot pizzas to Tigers fans stalled in traffic. They had a blast!

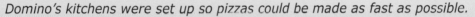

Domino's kitchens were set up so pizzas could be made as fast as possible.

All About Delivery

Monaghan opened his first **franchise** location in 1967. The first Domino's outside of Michigan opened in Burlington, Vermont, in 1968. The next year, he opened 32 stores.

At the same time, Monaghan continued improving his business. He helped to create the perfect pizza box. **Corrugated** cardboard made boxes strong enough to stack. Plus, the pizza was protected. Air vents kept pizzas hot and fresh instead of soggy from steam. Monaghan also **patented** an **insulating** pizza bag. Once again, this kept heat in but let moisture out.

Monaghan admired other successful food pioneers. So, he tried to figure out what made Domino's special. Colonel Harland Sanders had taken a simple recipe and built Kentucky Fried Chicken. Ray Kroc had practically invented the fast-food industry with McDonald's. Monaghan idolized those food giants. He knew Domino's needed an angle, something no one had done before. But what?

In the late 1960s, delivery service was not common. It was a courtesy, but no one had built success on it like Monaghan would. Monaghan's vision was all about pizza delivery! It was a solid concept. The special feature Monaghan was looking for had been part of the Domino's business all along.

Monaghan said his company was "built on wheels."

Pizza in 30

The 1970s were full of ups and downs. Starting in 1972, Monaghan called Ray Kroc every month. He asked if they could meet. The answer was always no.

In 1973, the Monaghan family moved into a beautiful new home in Ann Arbor. Then in 1975, Domino Sugar **sued** Domino's Pizza over their shared name. Domino's Pizza won in 1980. Judges ruled that no one would confuse pizza for sugar. Relieved, Monaghan burst into tears.

Just a few months later, Kroc said yes to a 15-minute meeting! It turned into two and a half hours of business advice from the McDonald's legend. That night, Monaghan got a call from a Domino's manager. Kroc had just walked in and ordered a pizza!

The 1980s were a time of major growth. In 1983, the first international stores opened in Canada and Australia. There were about 1,100 locations altogether.

In 1984, the company formalized its guarantee. Every pizza would be delivered hot and fresh in 30 minutes. In a peak year, 1985, 954 new stores opened to do just that. This included stores in the United Kingdom and Japan. The first South American Domino's opened in Colombia in 1988.

Monaghan was rich! He set out to fulfill his childhood dreams. He bought over 200 collector cars. He purchased houses designed by Frank Lloyd Wright. In 1983, he even bought his favorite baseball team, the Detroit Tigers. Then, the team won the 1984 World Series!

In 1973, Pizza Hut offered to buy Domino's. Flattered, Monaghan said no.

Success at Last

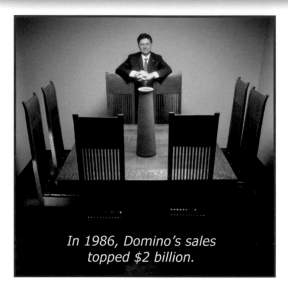

In 1986, Domino's sales topped $2 billion.

A big company needed a big headquarters. In 1984, Monaghan started building Domino's Farms. This huge office complex is in Ann Arbor. Its design honors Frank Lloyd Wright. By 1989, there were more than 5,000 Domino's locations. That year, the business added its first new menu item, Pan Pizza. Then in 1992, breadsticks became the first non-pizza menu item. Buffalo wings were introduced in 1994.

Despite his success, Monaghan was beginning to make major changes in his life. In 1992, he sold the Detroit Tigers. The owner of Little Caesars, another pizza chain, bought the team. Monaghan was realizing that possessions meant little without family, friends, and faith. He used his wealth to support causes he believed in. He donated money to political campaigns and to various organizations.

Bain Capital sold its interests in Domino's in 2010. That year, Patrick Doyle became CEO, the company opened its 9000th store, and it celebrated 50 years in business.

In 1993, Monaghan's business had to make a major change of its own. More than speedy delivery, Domino's valued safety. So, it dropped its 30-minute delivery guarantee. Instead, Domino's would remake pizzas or offer refunds to unhappy customers.

Domino's remained an established giant. But in 1998, Monaghan decided it was time to leave his business to other people. He sold Domino's to Bain Capital Inc.

Domino's Today

Today, more than 40 percent of Domino's orders are placed online.

Today, Domino's continues to offer many meal choices. The menu includes sub sandwiches, pasta, and chicken wings. Yet pizza is still the menu star. Domino's delivers up to 400 million pizzas a year.

Domino's supports more than 10,000 locations in more than 70 countries. The company employs 140,000 people. Its headquarters are still in Ann Arbor. Annual sales are over $7 billion worldwide.

Monaghan turned a small pizza place into a multibillion dollar business. When he left in 1998, he made another of his dreams come true. He founded what would become Ave Maria University in Ypsilanti. The Catholic school moved to Florida in 2003. There, Monaghan developed the town of Ave Maria. He designed the community to have homes, schools, a local government, and businesses.

With his successful pizza company, Monaghan changed the food industry. He made a success of his own life, too. He grew up with little but big dreams and an amazing work ethic. Monaghan is an American success and one awesome food dude!

In 2005, Monaghan was worth $500 million, but he pledged to give away much of that fortune.

Timeline

1937 Thomas Stephen Monaghan was born on March 25 near Ann Arbor, Michigan.

1955 Tom graduated from St. Thomas High School in Ann Arbor.

1959 Monaghan was discharged from the military.

1960 On December 9, Monaghan and his brother opened DomiNick's Pizza.

1961 Monaghan became the sole owner of DomiNick's.

1962 Monaghan married Marjorie Zybach on August 25.

1965 Monaghan named his pizza business Domino's.

1967 The first Domino's franchise opened.

1983 Domino's opened its first international stores; Monaghan bought the Detroit Tigers baseball team.

1984 Monaghan began building Domino's Farms.

1998 Monaghan sold Domino's; he founded what would become Ave Maria University.

Pizza Popularity

Tom Monaghan may not have cared for pizza the first time he tried it. But today, many people would disagree with that opinion! Pizza is extremely popular.

In the United States, 3 billion pizzas are sold every year.

That means 350 slices are sold every second!

The average American eats 46 slices in a year.

Pepperoni is the most popular pizza topping in the United States.

The next most popular toppings are mushrooms, sausage, ham, and green peppers.

Domino's alone delivers more than 1 million pizzas every day around the world.

Domino's pizza delivery drivers travel more than 10 million miles every week!

The busiest pizza delivery days are Super Bowl Sunday and Halloween.

Glossary

architect (AHR-kuh-tehkt) - a person who plans and designs buildings. His or her work is called architecture.

corrugated - having a wavy surface made of many folds.

debt (DEHT) - something owed to someone, especially money.

detention home - a place where children are kept, usually under the care of the court system.

foster care - a system that provides supervision and a place to live outside a person's regular home. Someone in foster care lives in a foster home.

franchise - the right granted to someone to sell a company's goods or services in a particular place. The business operating with this right is also known as a franchise.

grueling - very difficult, or requiring great effort.

insulate - to keep something from losing or transferring electricity, heat, or sound.

orphanage - a place for the care of children, usually those with no parents.

patent - to gain the exclusive right to make or sell an invention. This right lasts for a certain period of time.

peritonitis (pehr-uh-tuh-NEYE-tuhs) - an infection of the peritoneum, which lines the inner abdomen and organs.

seminary - a school where students study to be priests, ministers, or rabbis.

strict - following or demanding others to follow rules or regulations in a rigid, exact manner.

sue - to bring legal action against a person or an organization.

tuition (tuh-WIH-shuhn) - money students pay to receive instruction.

Websites

To learn more about Food Dudes,
visit **booklinks.abdopublishing.com**. These links are routinely monitored and updated to provide the most current information available.

Index

First Ladies

Dolley
Madison

Joanne Mattern

ABDO
Publishing Company

visit us at
www.abdopublishing.com

Published by ABDO Publishing Company, 8000 West 78th Street, Edina, Minnesota 55439.
Copyright © 2008 by Abdo Consulting Group, Inc. International copyrights reserved in all
countries. No part of this book may be reproduced in any form without written permission from the
publisher. The Checkerboard Library™ is a trademark and logo of ABDO Publishing Company.

Printed in the United States.

Cover Photo: Getty Images
Interior Photos: AP Images pp. 11, 19, 23, 24, 27; Corbis pp. 14, 21; Getty Images pp. 5, 17, 22, 25;
    Library of Congress pp. 6, 20; Macculloch Hall Historical Museum p. 15; North Wind pp. 7, 8,
    9, 10, 13, 16, 18

Series Coordinator: BreAnn Rumsch
Editors: Megan M. Gunderson, BreAnn Rumsch
Art Direction & Cover Design: Neil Klinepier

Library of Congress Cataloging-in-Publication Data

Mattern, Joanne, 1963-
  Dolley Madison / Joanne Mattern.
    p. cm. -- (First ladies)
  Includes index.
  ISBN-13: 978-1-59928-798-0
  1. Madison, Dolley, 1768-1849--Juvenile literature. 2. Presidents' spouses--United States--
Biography--Juvenile literature. I. Title.
  E342.1.M28 2007
  973.81092--dc22
  [B]
                                                                              2007009726

Contents

Dolley Madison

During her lifetime, Dolley Madison was one of the most famous women in the United States. She was married to James Madison, the nation's fourth president. The Madisons lived in the White House from 1809 to 1817.

President Madison adored his wife. So did the American people. Mrs. Madison loved to host parties and entertain guests. She was known as a charming hostess throughout her years in Washington, D.C.

During the **War of 1812**, Mrs. Madison rescued several national treasures from being destroyed. Her bravery led her to be regarded as a national hero.

Mrs. Madison's actions as First Lady set a strong example for future women who would fill the role. Today, she is remembered as a well respected and beloved First Lady. In fact, Mrs. Madison is considered one of the most popular First Ladies in U.S. history.

Dolley Madison was the best-loved First Lady of the 1800s.

A Happy Childhood

On May 20, 1768, Dolley Payne was born in Guilford County, North Carolina. Her parents, John and Mary Coles Payne, were happy to finally have a daughter. They already had two sons. Over the next several years, the Paynes had three more daughters and two more sons.

When Dolley was less than one year old, the family moved to Hanover County, Virginia. The Paynes lived on several different plantations there. They worked hard, but they lived well.

Since Dolley was the eldest daughter, she helped her mother with housekeeping and child care. The Paynes also had slaves who helped on the farm and did housework. One slave named Mother Amy looked after the Payne children.

When the Paynes moved to Virginia, they stayed at Scotchtown, their friend Patrick Henry's home. Mr. Henry later became the state's first governor.

Family time was important to the Paynes. They often sat around the fireplace after dinner. There, they shared stories and sang songs. Dolley's childhood was happy. She knew that her family loved her very much.

In the 1700s, cooking took much of the day. So, Dolley's chores were an important contribution to her family.

Life as a Quaker

The Paynes belonged to a religion called the **Society of Friends**. Members of this group are known as Quakers. John and Mary were important members of their church. They led meetings and kept records. Later, John became a Quaker preacher.

The Payne family attended their local Quaker meetings every month.

Quakers followed many **strict** rules. For example, they had to wear plain clothes. And, they were not allowed to play cards, dance, or attend public concerts or plays. They were only allowed to go to events put on by the Society of Friends. In addition, Quaker children were only permitted to play with other Quaker children.

However, Quakers believed that both girls and

boys should be educated. So like her brothers and sisters, Dolley attended a Quaker school. There, she learned to read and write.

Dolley enjoyed school. But, she did not like the other rules of her religion. She liked parties and pretty, colorful clothes. As Dolley grew older, she had a difficult time following the rules.

Dolley was lucky to attend school. At that time, girls usually stayed home to help with chores.

War!

When Dolley was eight years old, the **American Revolution** began. Many battles took place in Virginia, near her home. But, the Quaker religion did not allow its members to fight in the war. So, Dolley's father and brothers did not join the military.

As the war progressed, many laws were changed. One change pleased the Paynes very much. In 1782, Virginia passed a law that said slaveholders could choose to free their slaves. So, the Paynes made a big decision. They freed all of their slaves, because owning slaves went against Quaker beliefs.

However, it soon became impossible to run the plantation without any help. So in 1783, the Paynes sold their land and moved to Philadelphia, Pennsylvania. Dolley was about to begin a new life in the big city!

American colonists in every part of the country wanted to join the Revolution.

10

Each year at Christmas, reenactors march to Washington Crossing, Pennsylvania. There, they re-create George Washington's famous crossing of the Delaware River during the American Revolution.

A New Home

Dolley was 15 years old when her family moved to a small house in Philadelphia. There, her father started a new business selling laundry starch. Although the family was comfortable, living in a crowded city was difficult at first. Life there was very different from the country life Dolley was used to.

At the time, Philadelphia was the nation's capital. In 1783, about 40,000 people were living there. The city had schools, a large hospital, a theater, markets, and beautiful gardens. Dolley loved to watch people walking in the streets. She especially enjoyed seeing women wearing fancy gowns. Dolley wished she could dress like that, too.

Philadelphia was also home to many Quakers. So, Dolley had plenty of friends. She loved going to picnics, tea parties, meetings, and other social events.

In 1786, Dolley met a young law student named John Todd Jr. He was a Quaker, just like Dolley. John fell in love with her right away. Dolley liked spending time with John. However, she was not yet ready to get married.

During the late 1700s, Philadelphia was the second-largest U.S. city. Today, many famous buildings from Dolley's lifetime still stand.

Hard Times

In Philadelphia, the Payne family endured some hardships. Mary gave birth to another daughter. Sadly, the baby died a few months later. Then, Dolley's older brother Walter sailed to England. The family never saw him again.

In 1789, John's business went **bankrupt**. The Quakers were angry at John for not paying his bills. So, he was banned from attending Quaker meetings. And, Mary had to take in boarders to earn money for the family.

Through these difficult times, John Todd was always by Dolley's side. In 1790, they were married in a simple Quaker ceremony. The **newlyweds** remained in Philadelphia, where John ran a successful law office.

In 1791, the couple moved into a larger home. And in February 1792, they welcomed their first child, John Payne. Dolley decided to call him Payne. She happily cared for her new family.

Dolley enjoyed being lady of the house during her marriage to John.

However, 1793 turned out to be a terrible year. Many people in Philadelphia became sick with **yellow fever**. Dolley and John had a second son, William Temple, in September. Tragically, John and the baby both died of the disease on October 24. Dolley was a widow at just 25 years old.

John Todd

Outbreak!

For the residents of Philadelphia, Pennsylvania, 1793 was a horrible year. In the spring, the city received a lot of rain. The summer was especially hot. These conditions allowed mosquitoes to lay more eggs than normal. Then, new residents came from tropical climates, bringing yellow fever with them. Soon, the city's large mosquito population became infected and rapidly spread the disease.

The city's doctors did not know what to do! They advised healthy people to flee the city. So, many families were separated. It is estimated that between 2,000 and 4,000 people died that summer. This was equal to 10 percent of Philadelphia's population at that time.

The Philadelphia epidemic was the largest in American history. The infections finally stopped in November, when frost killed off the mosquitoes.

Today, yellow fever is rarely a problem in America. This is because the disease is prevented with a vaccine. Children receive the vaccine at a very young age. Unfortunately, many tropical parts of the world still experience yellow fever. So, it will always be important to use the vaccine.

Meeting James

Dolley missed John very much. Thankfully, he had left her with enough money to live comfortably. Dolley and her son Payne stayed in Philadelphia. Soon, Dolley's 14-year-old sister, Anna, moved in with them. Slowly, life returned to normal.

Dolley had many friends who were important members of the government. One of them was a man named Aaron Burr. One day, Aaron introduced Dolley to his friend James Madison.

Dolley enjoyed meeting James. He was 17 years older than she was. James was also a wealthy, well-educated

Many people called James "the Great Little Madison." This is because he was only 66 inches (168 cm) tall.

congressman from Virginia. He had helped write the U.S. **Constitution** and the **Bill of Rights**. James liked Dolley very much. But, he was shy. So, he wrote Dolley many letters.

Soon, James asked Dolley to marry him. Everyone in Philadelphia was talking about the couple and their romance. On September 15, 1794, Dolley and James were happily married.

Dolley had her portrait painted just weeks after she and James wed.

A Political Wife

Mr. Madison was not a Quaker. So after they married, Mrs. Madison had to leave the **Society of Friends**. She did not really mind. She no longer had to follow **strict** rules about plain dress. Now she could wear the fashionable, pretty clothes she loved.

In 1800, Washington, D.C., became the capital of the United States. That same year, Thomas Jefferson was elected the third U.S. president. He named Mr. Madison the **secretary of state**. This was an important government position. The Madisons moved to Washington, D.C., in May 1801.

President Jefferson also needed a hostess for political gatherings. His wife had died many years earlier. So, he asked Mrs. Madison for her help. Since she loved giving parties, she was happy to agree.

Thomas Jefferson was a good friend to the Madisons.

Mrs. Madison invited many different people to the president's parties. Sometimes, these people disagreed over political issues. But when they argued, Mrs. Madison quickly changed the subject so her guests would not fight. She had a talent for putting people at ease. Soon, she was the most popular woman in Washington.

Mrs. Madison's charm and sense of humor made her guests feel warmly welcomed.

A New Sense of Style

The Madisons remained important in Washington throughout President Jefferson's term. On March 4, 1809, Mr. Madison became the fourth president of the United States. Americans were glad Mrs. Madison was the new First Lady. People liked and admired her for many reasons. She respected different opinions on political issues and treated everyone equally. And, she was very proud of her country.

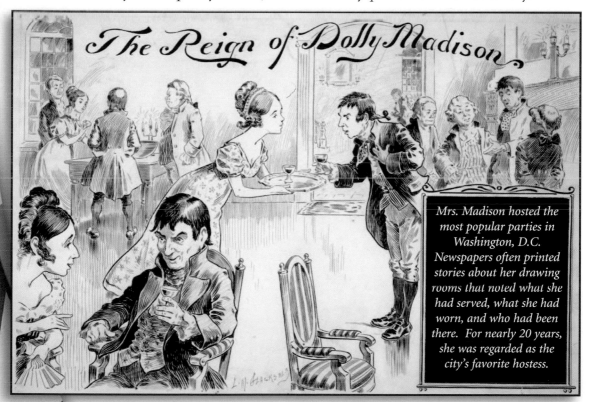

The Reign of Dolly Madison

Mrs. Madison hosted the most popular parties in Washington, D.C. Newspapers often printed stories about her drawing rooms that noted what she had served, what she had worn, and who had been there. For nearly 20 years, she was regarded as the city's favorite hostess.

Many people looked to the president and his home for ideas about entertaining. The First Lady hosted parties, government dinners, and other events. She welcomed guests almost every night. Usually, she entertained government officials and other important figures.

But on Wednesdays, Mrs. Madison opened her parties to the public. These gatherings were called "drawing rooms." The First Lady made each guest feel welcome. And, everyone was treated with respect.

Mrs. Madison also helped decorate the President's House. Later, this building would be called the White House. The First Lady was more stylish than anyone! She loved to wear fancy gowns, gloves, slippers, hats, and jewelry. Some people said Mrs. Madison dressed like a queen.

The British are Coming!

Shortly before President Madison was reelected in 1812, the United States entered a difficult time. The country became involved in the **War of 1812**, a conflict with Great Britain. On August 19, 1814, British soldiers marched toward Washington, D.C. By August 24, the president had decided to meet with the U.S. army.

Mrs. Madison and a few others stayed at the President's House. But later that day, she heard British cannons firing on the city. The First Lady did not want important government papers to fall into British hands. So she acted quickly. She packed many papers and other belongings into a wagon and left the capital city.

The First Lady's courage saved many national treasures from the flames.

British soldiers reached the President's House soon after Mrs. Madison had left. In fact, they sat down to the hot meal she had prepared for her husband! After their dinner, the soldiers burned the house and many other government buildings.

Stuart's portrait contains meaningful symbols about America.

A National Hero

Mrs. Madison is the only First Lady who has had to face an invasion of the White House! However, she handled the crisis with quick thinking. Mrs. Madison packed as many treasures as she could. She made sure to rescue her husband's papers and a copy of the Declaration of Independence. She also took some curtains and the blue and gold set of china she had purchased for state dinners.

Mrs. Madison especially wanted to rescue a large painting of George Washington. Hurriedly, she had her servants break the frame, pull out the painting, and roll it up. Mrs. Madison left the city by carriage, just minutes before the British troops arrived.

The portrait of George Washington was painted by Gilbert Stuart, an important American artist. He created four similar paintings, known today as the Lansdowne portraits. Without Mrs. Madison's fast thinking, the painting would most likely have been destroyed in the fire.

Today, the painting is well protected by the Smithsonian Institute, one of America's most important museums. The painting represents important ideas about the United States at the time it was painted. It remains one of the nation's oldest and most valued treasures.

Alone Once More

After the British soldiers left Washington, D.C., the Madisons returned to the capital. However, they had to stay in a friend's home while the President's House was rebuilt.

On December 24, 1814, the United States and Great Britain signed the Treaty of Ghent. This ended the **War of 1812**. For the next two years, President Madison and other politicians rebuilt

Montpelier was surrounded by hills and filled with beautiful flower gardens.

Washington, D.C. Mrs. Madison kept their spirits up by hosting parties and drawing rooms.

On March 4, 1817, President Madison finished his second term in office. The Madisons retired to Montpelier, their plantation near Richmond, Virginia. Mr. Madison spent most days writing letters. Mrs. Madison helped him organize his political papers. In the evenings, they entertained guests and hosted many dinner parties.

Mr. and Mrs. Madison loved each other very much.

Mrs. Madison remained connected to friends in Washington, D.C., during her husband's retirement.

Mrs. Madison once wrote, "Our hearts understand each other." As the years passed, her husband's health began to fail. Sadly, Mr. Madison died at Montpelier on June 28, 1836. Mrs. Madison was a widow for the second time. She was comforted by the many letters she received.

A Life Remembered

After her husband died, Mrs. Madison wanted to publish his presidential papers. In April 1837, Congress bought some of the papers and published them. Soon after, Mrs. Madison returned to Washington, D.C., where many of her friends still lived. She began attending parties and dinners again.

Still, Mrs. Madison often visited Montpelier. She had trusted her son Payne to run the plantation. Unfortunately, he did such a poor job that she was forced to sell the estate in 1844. Later, Congress published the rest of Mr. Madison's papers. This raised enough money for Mrs. Madison to live comfortably in Washington, D.C., for the rest of her life.

By summer 1849, Mrs. Madison's health was poor. She died at home on July 12, surrounded by friends and family. Thousands of people mourned her death. Her funeral procession was the largest the city had ever seen. As a special honor, Mrs. Madison was buried in the Congressional Cemetery. However, her body was later moved to the cemetery at Montpelier.

Dolley Madison's spirit, grace, and charm have been remembered long after her death. Today, she remains one of America's most popular and famous First Ladies. Mrs. Madison will always be remembered for changing the role of First Lady. She became an example of how a First Lady can support her husband, as well as her country and its people.

Though she was First Lady for only eight years, Mrs. Madison was recognized as an important political figure for more than 50 years.

Timeline

1768	Dolley Payne was born on May 20.
1783	Dolley's family moved to Philadelphia, Pennsylvania.
1790	Dolley married John Todd Jr.
1792	Dolley and John's son John Payne was born in February.
1793	Dolley and John's son William Temple was born in September; on October 24, John and baby William both died of yellow fever.
1794	Dolley married James Madison on September 15.
1801	Mr. Madison became secretary of state; the Madisons moved to Washington, D.C.; Mrs. Madison began acting as President Jefferson's official hostess.
1809–1817	Mrs. Madison acted as First Lady, while her husband served as president.
1814	Mrs. Madison rescued important documents and national treasures from the President's House on August 24.
1836	Mr. Madison died on June 28.
1837	Mrs. Madison sold some of her husband's presidential papers to Congress to be published.
1849	Mrs. Madison died on July 12.

Did You Know?

Though her parents recorded her name at birth, Dolley has mistakenly been called Dolly, as well as Dorothy or Dorthea, throughout the years.

Due to her popularity as a hostess, many food companies have used Dolley Madison's name to sell their products, such as ice cream, cookies, popcorn, and doughnuts.

Mrs. Madison was the first First Lady to attend a presidential inauguration in Washington, D.C.

Mrs. Madison was the first woman to redecorate the White House.

In 1812, Mrs. Madison made the arrangements for the first wedding held at the White House. There, her sister Lucy married Supreme Court Justice Thomas Todd.

Mrs. Madison purchased the White House's first piano and first collection of music. Unfortunately, these items were destroyed in the 1814 fire.

Mrs. Madison owned a green parrot named Polly.

After Mr. Madison died, Congress granted Mrs. Madison a lifetime seat on the floor of the House of Representatives. This was the highest honor ever given to a president's widow.

Glossary

American Revolution - from 1775 to 1783. A war for independence between Great Britain and its North American colonies. The colonists won and created the United States of America.

bankrupt - legally declared unable to pay debts.

Bill of Rights - a summary of rights in the U.S. Constitution that the United States guarantees to the American people.

Constitution - the laws that govern the United States.

newlywed   a person who just married.

secretary of state - a member of the president's cabinet who handles relations with other countries.

Society of Friends - a Christian group first developed in England during the 1600s, in opposition to the Catholic Church. Followers reject worldly goods and honors, believing instead that all people are equal to receive the word of God.

strict - demanding others to follow rules or regulations in a rigid, exact manner.

War of 1812 - from 1812 to 1814. A war fought between the United States and Great Britain over shipping rights and the capture of U.S. soldiers.

yellow fever - a disease transmitted by the yellow-fever mosquito, usually in warm climates. It is marked by fever, headache, yellow-colored skin, and internal bleeding.

Web Sites

To learn more about Dolley Madison, visit ABDO Publishing Company on the World Wide Web at **www.abdopublishing.com**. Web sites about Dolley Madison are featured on our Book Links page. These links are routinely monitored and updated to provide the most current information available.

Index